I AM NOT YOUNG

AND I WILL DIE

WITH THIS CAR

IN MY GARAGE

I AM NOT YOUNG AND I WILL DIE WITH THIS CAR IN MY GARAGE

poems

BLAKE Z. RONG

atmosphere press

Published by Atmosphere Press

Author photo by Kevin McCauley
Cover design by Andrea Streeter

atmospherepress.com

TABLE OF CONTENTS

*It is difficult but necessary to accept
the truth of what we are at our
loneliest moments.*

-Jim Harrison

Sino-Soviet Split

The Committee believes that we are no good for each other.
The Politburo has issued a statement
from the party line to your ears:
our borders are irreconcilable, tensing in relations.
We fell short of the Five Year Plan.
We failed the goals of the General Assembly.
They have adjusted the targets to offset the loss,
sniffed out the traitors and had them all shot.
The radios have fallen silent. The troops
are in the streets, and the chairman's head
is up against the wall. The papers scream:
through all citizens in constant revolution
the Party and the Union shall prevail.
There will be no further statements at this time.

But we have left scars on each other's bodies
deep and overflowing with rolling pitch black
like the floodplains naked. Burn marks across the skin
like collapsing houses. At the riverbed
where we once held hands, we watch the tanks
as they creak across simple bridges,
brave and halting first steps to new homelands:
every inch a declaration,
every mile a door kicked open.
Gathering so much sand in the gears,
the movement grinds noisily to a halt
like a soldier shot upon the steppes
realizing that it's too late to turn back, turn back.
Let some dusty comrade give him a hero's return.

The End of the World Exploratory Committee

We are seagrass and white foam, we are
the shrieking of seagulls this far inland,
we are plastic bags caressed from flimsy trash bins
released once again into the wild
            where we
belong.

We are at the mercy of our prey. I want
to be a cat like water,
to slink into any form, shape-shifting
            naked and hungry
            eyes open like saucers
            pulling my knees to my chest

teeth and claws sunk into my temples.

Filtering through bookshelves listening for breath
jumping at the sound of unlocking doors
houseflies drawn to the smell of my sweat
I press my eyelids closed
like squeezing blood
from quiet stones.

Here, let me try again—
fueled by sweat and lubricated with
pauper's blood, inking the corners
of dark rooms left bare, vulnerable to
material resonance. Our skin is hungry.
Our enemies will greet me
with howls of hatred.
Who will raise the first stone?
Who will be the cause of all my regret?
Who will sing bird songs at the end of the world?

There are particular American cruelties
hard-wired into our veins. Watch me,
just watch me
            catch this rubber bullet between my teeth.
Human treasures captured for all eternity
stuffed and mounted for our slack-jawed posterity
because our ears still ring with their damned batons.
We want life, we seek breath, but
we expect calamity.
Give us another reason to break.

We see you, we hear you,
but we can neither confirm nor deny.

This is the end, we have confirmed. Our instruments
have never lied. The ships arise from the ocean floor and
the ghosts that haunt your building are coming back
to collect their rent and the memories of the dead
will brush your skin as they walk past you
on darkened streets.

The Legend of the East Village Skylark

Great grinning teeth, street light shining through
bent and crumpled bars, you don't sing too loud anymore
with your crooked eye, your sneering lips. Nose bent in
like a third-rate boxer. Your three battered shields
red white and blue once meant something
akin to pride, perhaps. Every scar across
your stamped metal flanks
tells a story of how you escaped,
time and time again

and it is not up to us to decide how mundane it is.

Nobody walks past your sealed-beam lights
singing *look out honey, cuz I'm using technology.*
Do they know, you think? About a city that
eats its young like a mother cat,
shielding and subjecting her newborns to
this cruel and reckless world—

police horses in Tompkins Square Park
dragging the leering freaks away
from the warmth of their fires. Brothers-in-arms
half-sunken and battered in the East River mud.
Running the length down Stillwell Avenue
dodging strollers, trying to make the connection—

of some history unfathomable
written in sans-serif fonts
as weary platitudes in salad bar chains.
A rich man's city, gritty yet iridescent,
where the past is repaved
with translucent amber and concrete dust.

But we will
        return to you,
you golden thing, us wool-winged moths
to embers ablaze,
and when you lie for the count

you see a sky unblinking, no future to divine, no
history entombed, and somewhere beyond
the hazy lights the night sky is

        full of stars.

Cloud, Castle, Sea

In Dalian where the mountains drop down
into the edge of the Yellow Sea, you will find

a miniature Versailles, a Hall of Mirrors,
Eiffel Towers and châteaus, Duomos and piazzas,

Canałassos and Pontes de Rialto over still concrete pools,
entombed in ice where the skate lines cross. Plastic bottles

jutting out like icebergs. Each building a shell defiant against
rusty battleships and forlorn theme parks and time and space.

Emptied, this late season, under slate-grey clouds.
Press your nose against the glass. Witness dust and plywood

    like the gaps between stitches that you can never sew
    up.

From the castle over Xinghai Bay, gilded in
wrought-iron tigers and *fleur de lys*, one's private

Neuschwanstein, nineteen floors up, facing
superhighways and suspension bridges,

the mouths of the tunnel bound for
parts unknown, nowhere here, nowhere else,

all is past and gone. Truly great men
look to this age alone—but you

outrun your own history long enough
and you end up in someone else's past.

Song for Neo-Tokyo in the Year of its Destruction

Have you got color in your cheeks?
Do you hear the silence on the other end?
You discover that you are made of flowers.
At a press conference King Ghidorah apologizes for the
     rampage,
bowing his three heads before the podium.
Today we will paint a mountain that owes us nothing.
Come up for air, come out of Shibuya station
thinking foolishly that's real air you're breathing:
tomorrow the tabby cats will whisper directions
to the floor in Seibu where the gemstones are hidden.
Thin plastic films reflect the coming disaster.
Plucked on a whale string, the city becomes human in its
     unraveling.
Do you hear the silence on the other end?
Have you got color in your cheeks?

DEATH FOR DRUG TRAFFICKERS UNDER SINGAPORE LAW

Vermont will always remind me
of heartbreak. But so will New Haven,
      and Austin,
and Port Henry, more recent than not.
There is

no sense in this great migration if
you're going to bring it all
with you anyway,
      instead of leaving it
at the curb for the Goodwill truck

but no, you carry it like so much
checked luggage that chafes the
shoulder blades, suitcases of
glass and India Ink and discarded bones
sense memories of chicharrones
gorgon stares from mermaid lions,
teargas and peony leaves and gathering clouds

and you pass it through the X-ray
like it's no big deal
Like you already have
      an explanation
bubbling at your lips. *No sir,*

*I cannot possibly
open this bag.* You see, this is
      part of my body now,

fused to my spine, growing from
the tips of my fingers
wrapped around
the leather straps.

Please, pat me down again. Brush the back
of your hand upward until you
            feel resistance.
Did a stranger pack your bags? Did a man or woman
ask you to carry something for them?
A piece of their absence?
A small good thing?
A little kiss?

Yes sir, I'll come this way. I'm ready for my close-up. A long time
      ago
someone asked me to hold onto this—

long black tendrils
swirling inside the body scanner,
          gathering smoke.

Hangover Poem, Newport Rhode Island

There are the days when you wake up

and the air dances in front of your eyes

in all its silk-charged finery: bands of dust

in the skies, musk of concrete and erupting dirt

ground-up asphalt underneath the jackhammers

open garbage cans, smoke of diesel

to choke us in our sleep. A Harley rumbles past

and makes a right onto Thames, so loud and screaming,

yet angry at nothing. There is comfort from mulch,

its cherry and spice, tang of brine

and seaweed

and a seagull's shit.

This morning a bloated belly stared back from the mirror,

grinning wickedly and taunting me *you drink any more beer*

you'll turn into a molasses barrel and you'll flood the whole town,

exploding onto the earth below. Oh Lord, I subject this

temple of a body to war crimes—

napalm, firebombing, the razing of ghettos.

Yet I am fortunate not to feel physical pain.

And in the square by Touro Street

I had once lain on the cobblestones,

under the stars,

what little stars that

I could see.

Miami, 1994

Down on the street all you gorgeous bodies
vibrate against each other like

supercharged miracles, high tension wires
buzzing humming arcing across

the small of your backs in the silken air all
potential energy about to burst.

All this town is

    is

    bored listless cat eyes
    framed in neon day-glo wattage

    soft afternoon rains and hard dusky rains
    purple hazy majesties, night sky and dark seas

blending like a wall of house paint. From my window
on the second story I am

king and kingdom intertwined, I am

that much closer to god. Red neon scatters
across the parking lot and raindrops penetrate

the swimming pools and the stray cats squat upon the stairs
but I don't get spooked no more. In the breakwater I hold

onto nothing. Yet I want all that ghosts want—
a peach pit in my heart, wrapped in twine.

Sometimes the Atlantic roars and howls like
the animal it is, a wide blue continent, fearful and alive.

15

The hotline says: *girls are waiting to talk to you.*
The VCR is set to auto-rewind. Asia Carrera bleats out

her last orgasm and the machine clicks on and
the telephone dial blinks *No new messages,*

press 0 to connect to an outside line. Claw marks

in the clouds from passing jets reveal pink and blue.
I miss the age when I still feared ghosts.

and when I pick
up the phone,
there'll be
nobody home.

Gabinetto Segreto

we are a pair of gutshot iguanas.
we speak
in one hour.

we are Black Guard Impermanence.
before the gates
of ghost cities
fearful white maples
magpies in rain.

grant me this graceful aura
among crypts of skulls
bleating of goats
how the hours
add up.

phantom rings in my left leg
postcards as permanent as a gun

dogsick for days
back to the noise of it all

and you
a secret museum
a song

Chaos Theories

There are no off-world colonies. Therefore: fuck it, take up
smoking. Grow your hair out. Move to Berlin. Adopt a dozen cats.
Feed them skin cells you flense off your forearms. Listen to
GG Allin, embrace the crust in your beard. Shit or piss into a
post office box, tuck razor blades under your tongue,
bury cinderblocks under neat piles of leaves,
recite inaccurate theories on entropy
to your friends who will put on airs
up and down Karl-Marx-Straße
as you surround yourself with
threats from minor deities
and bar napkin scribbles
and Bundt cake recipes
and you move like
light, swift
and silent
across the
panopticon
of our stars,
because every symphony
is a suicide postponed.

Morning Fog In Singapore

flasks of cheap gin
behind the counter
at 7-Eleven in the
basement of the Orchard Mall
toward Dhoby Ghaut station
where just like here
as well as back there
you avoid eye contact
shouting over thunderclaps
that stopped bringing rain
in the late year. it's 92
degrees and the cotton
is supposed to breathe,
to cover the shame
of your hairless chest,
your absent heart,
the ache of your rosy longing.

***

dream of a day where you wake up
not remembering you could be dying
blowing the blood out of your nose
talking to civilians without the waft
of flames lapping from your tongue
wishing it would last all day; this instinct
stumbling into these little adventures
where you don't know the language
but you know passion:

*I believe maybe poetry demands a
certain drunkenness, wouldn't you say?*

the thunder never rumbles
but actually booms, explodes,
the way we are led to believe. consider
the 2,200 plant species in Singapore alone—
Simpoh Lak and lipstick,
the broad leaves of wax flowers,
Seashore Purslane and *Freycinetia javanica;*
Consider recipes for soy sauce chicken and
barbequed stingray,
nasi briyani and chili crab,
Westerners touting Michelin stars in
the only approval that matters. in a hundred years
all this will be underwater, all this will be
salt water lapping against
the balustrades of the Fullerton Hotel
corroding rose-gold Cartiers
in their display cases and
plugging the cannons at
Fort Canning Park and
the gondolas that ply
the concrete canals of Marina Bay Sands
from the casino
to Bottega Veneta, well,
clearly they'll have seen this coming.

    ***

the cashier beams with joy
(for some reason) when your

credit card goes through and you,
with animal instincts,
baseline discrepancies,
alone among millions,
free from glaring eyes
and moral hygiene spectres—
well, this is one thing
you won't have to worry about
when the storm clouds break.

You have to start by tricking yourself. One day you might dig up some evil from a past life, give it a good polish, and become a swindler in this one.

-Yoko Tawada, "To Zagreb"

Khrushchev Trying to Enter Disneyland

The situation is inconceivable. The American authorities
cannot guarantee my safety. I love God, my family,
and my country. I have high blood pressure. What will they
tell me that they haven't already? Teach me curse words
in your language, get me on the horn to Moscow.
The petulant son has arrived before the kingdom:
I came to see distant gauzy visions, the skintight suits
of merriment, falling like dragons, I am owed my stomach
in my throat. Sound the alarms, fire the signal flares.
My comrades are in disbelief. What do I tell them?
Is there an epidemic of cholera? Do you have
    rocket-launching pads there?
Have gangsters taken over the place that can destroy me?

Now I tongue the cyanide pill of my secrets
before the gates of the happiest place on Earth.

At Eternity's Gate

Did Van Gogh ever fuck? Listen: don't tell me. I could
          probably look this up, but I'm too lazy. Instead, I'll
just go by the look on his face, that lost expression

hidden in his hands—old man, his bald head smooth
          like a computer mouse, balling mashed-potato fists into
where the eye sockets go. We see, but we cannot listen. All we
     can do

is fill in the blanks. Vibrating alongside the strings he plucks
          for us. Did he know? That he would be loved, and make
love, and lose love, and chase love through

fields of wheat and trodden cow paths, the crows soaring
          their black-bodied wings into pale jagged light
somewhere north of Auvers, zig-zagging up the hills?

Spoilers, sweetie. I long for the words that will
          prove me wrong: turning away from the tintype
with my face pinched—wispy, a blur, a ghost. That first year

in the village I tried to not look lonely in restaurants.
          I stared at a lot of mirrors
in dim public bathrooms. Lying on the hardwood

in a stranger's house. Hugging my knees to my chest in the
     shower,
          I invented a language
that would unravel my fists, pull my face back up, heavy-laden
     with

what it saw. Not an artist but a fully-formed creature,

        worthy of God's attention,
capable of multitudes.

But a heart that is shattering
        makes a beautiful sound.
                    25

The Good Kind

I ain't the good kind of Asian. I'm the one
who disappoints you. I see it in your eyes

when we go out for sushi and I forget what nigiri is.
I feel it across your tattoos I'll kiss someday:

koi fish samurai and fisherman's wives
wide-eyed cats with claws outstretched

characters faded indecipherable, strewn like wreckage
across your arms. And someday I too will be

dissolved in lost-wax vaporwave
neon and pink and crystalline

clad in red and yellow camouflage. Listen!
My people were pulled from the dirt

among the botflies and the rifle butts
feigning death, deep in the surface of the earth

before they embarked on the long march

their feet sore their bellies aching
knowing the pain but no potential

then self-destructing like strings of firecrackers.

Knowing the words but not the melody. Let me teach you
the curse words of my language. I will flip through pages

of dictionary tracing them into my skin with a crimson pen.

Someday I'll learn how to pronounce them right.

Sometime we'll all do our parents proud.

Somewhere out there Alphonse is still trapped
     in that endless suit of armor.

Lament for the Accidental Killer of Camille Jenatzy

> *Camille Jenatzy, the first man to break the 100 km/h barrier in 1899...died in a hunting accident. He went behind a bush and made animal noises as a prank on his friends. Alfred Madoux fired, believing it was a wild animal. They rushed him to hospital by car; he bled to death en route, fulfilling his own prophecy he would die in a Mercedes.*

How was I to know this was all
an elaborate joke, this weak and weary life,
grasping at morsels, grasping at anything
that called from the bushes, laid neatly
within my sights: this fortune from God,
this tantalizing hope? Bestow us this dream of
a reward. You: the great *Diable Rouge*, your
great grinning smile, framed by curls the color of fire
emerging from a rifle's barrel, this burst of
animal electricity, faster, faster,
faster than anyone: you had found a way
to make a great farce of it all, to
end the century on your own terms.

You, who once felt the kiss of speed
aiming for the blue-inked horizon—
you peered at boilers and magnetos,
pistons and tillers and battery coils
and you asked if there was more to this, to this
great and painless world, carried by the
high-tension current of now. On that day in Achères
you hit your marks. You knew
that it would not last, this spectre
of history, spectacle of fame,
elegant sweat of genius: charging pulsing
restless yearning through the night,
the moon unbowing.

From the lodge at Habay la Neuve
we rushed you to the ambulance.
No time, no time. What was it
that you once said, friend? You would die
in a Mercedes, you had laughed, someday,
someday after the great victory. So we
followed a star on the nose, watching your
eyes unblinking, staring, realizing:
one minute, forty seconds. All it took
to stare down infinite universes
knowing that there was no realm
where you could be satisfied.

Impala

Pregnant: belly bulging out like a soap bubble,
taped up elbow, bandages
stained with dirt and dried blood
from a fall upon a fall; how clumsy can you be
when there's someone riding shotgun?
Barrel of a faucet to lean against,
to take the strain off your curved back,
among the thick trees blurry out of sight,
branches heavy with dying leaves,
almost like late summer
somewhere out there
somewhere in the places where
people drive past
and barely turn their heads
and go tsk in their mouths
clicking their tongues
against their movie star teeth.

What do you not see?
Outside of the frame, invisible:
a creature of indiscriminate breed.
A Chevrolet Impala on cinderblocks.
Army issue equipment from a fake war.
A thousand of panes of glass, shattering simultaneously.

Who taught you to fear that?
Beauty and destruction in one fell swoop.
Give the sound of a dog's supplicating breath
to a woman who is grieving her mother
in dead-ended pathways unfolding
like paper fortune tellers: left right up down
a thousand years under the flap. A dark-haired loon

who could not stay for the feature presentation
who found herself carried out by the ushers
unruly and defiant
before the lights come back up
and her eyes went dark;
before the spectacle hits like a car
headed toward the offramp.
I kept the red vinyl so pure, so buttery soft.
A tiger's never going to change its stripes.

A&P

I loved you like a dead novelist
loves his metaphor of America
while wandering the supermarket shelves:
along bounties of lettuce and strawberries,
past kettle chips and boxes of spaghetti,
aisles of Italian Mexican *International*
shuffling his cart with filets of salmon
trimmed neatly with all the bones
removed for your convenience.

He sees bathing-suit girls
at the checkout counter. They
stare blankly at the parking lot
waiting for the Pontiac Catalina
to pull up with their boyfriends in tow
just for the summer and one summer only.

Rose-peach cheeks and zucchini noses,
flowers across our faces, squinting cloves for eyes.
They knew that we could never last the year.
Everything good and beautiful is eventually
wrapped in plastic.

There Will Be A Song For When They Find Your Body

For Davey G. Johnson

fast as a shark,
who wanted it
way too loud,
your god
an angry god,

you were incandescent—
a flame-kissed tear in a
Sierra Nevada wind
forty degrees Fahrenheit
and dropping. you climbed
California State Route 49
in sun-soaked plastic,
an aluminum trellis,
atop nine hundred ninety-eight
cubic centimeters
of raw whining power

while the sun cast its
final warmth of the day
upon the ghosts of cannibals.

you were not without scars
on your brain and your body:
you had felt grief like
a new limb, the void of
an absent hand
whose movements
you could still quite grasp.
you had screamed through
sheets of drywall in San Pedro,
bracing yourself against

the salt-water spray,
yet you always knew
what time it was,
stainless-steel Rolex
a kaleidoscope curse.

on the day you turned from the current
you cast a gaze at the North Fork below
where the ducks take flight
like silent seaplanes, two in a row—
hadn't you heard once
that they mated for life?
the last creatures
on Earth, you must have
said to her on the day you proposed,
in the Four Seasons lobby
in Ferragamo slippers—

apologies, please. but these memories
flood my bones in your stead.

like circling Lake Tahoe,
my first few desperate miles
across the divining lines;

four in the morning, watching you
through the windshield
as you held a lover
before these headlights;

before we dropped down
to San Francisco Bay.
we flew airplanes in your backyard.
that morning I had driven
from Playa Del Rey,

all staircase wit in your
ranch-style house,
and I believed back then
that my friends would last forever—

that rushing water
wouldn't dissolve
your body
cell by cell

wispy and white like egg drop soup.

all rage ends pointed to the skies
for it knows not what echoes through its
negative space. from this void
we expect no answers,
commit no faults,
and we can blame no one else.

(not the Sausage Creature,
not the Year of The Goose.)

maybe the future is coming,
maybe it was written in your stars,

and when they find your body
we will sing
what we had sung all along.

what we say in the spaces between words

the worst thing someone ever told me
is that there is no "Moe"
behind "Moe's Southwest Grille"
but instead an acronym
that stands for

       musicians

               outlaws

       and entertainers

—

the second worst thing someone ever told me
was that "despair" sounds like
"j'espere," *I hope*,
a saccharine sentiment if anything;
too weak to connect the dots
like something akin to

      long-lost constellations

      a candlestick in the drawing room

      or a burning fuse

when a man is drowning
you don't throw a rope
and tie it to thin air

Lament for the Yuba County 5

*On Feb. 24, 1978, five mentally disabled men from 40 miles north
of Sacramento vanished into the night on their way home from a
Chico State basketball game. More than 100 days passed before
the snow melted and search parties found four of the boys' bodies
in rugged Plumas National Forest. At least one had survived for
weeks in a remote forest service trailer nearly 20 miles from his
group's car. Body parts of the others were found nearby.*

you
roll the windows down
emerge from steel cocoons
leave mercury behind

you
in disdainful terrain
seeking polaris
but they all point north

you
in heartache throes
watching for flashlights
may death arrive via trolley

you
thirteen weeks later:
your steel wool beard
your neglected cornucopias

your skull
below your spine
300 feet away
wind howling absent cartilage

you
without shoes
wandering bare ground
in perpetuity

Midnight In Italian

Across rumpled bedsheets

we explore each other's scars

and pluck the white hair out of our scalps.

Our lips are wet with the evidence. Let all

the mosquitos die their painful deaths.

—

Unknown engines

chrome and gleaming

vibrate behind bloodshot eyes

as we explore each other's bodies

nervously, like Vesuvio in the dark

faces turned skyward in permanent grace.

Even an absence of love contains

its possibility. High-test tigers in our bellies,

mouthfuls of dead languages on our tongues:

my nose tucked in the curve of your neck,

your memory the route to my childhood home.

Fallen Cosmonaut

For Vladimir Komarov

1.

Catch me with a bullet between my teeth. I'm magic,
swerving on the sidewalk like it's the Puerto Rican parade,
like I'm swinging a pocketwatch from a gold chain
from my snakeskin belt. Listen baby—I'm Superfly TNT
I'm the Guns of the Navarone a bad Moto Guzzi
       a bat's crystal wing that's gone, long gone
before that crimson morning comes.
Listen baby—I'm on that death trip like Iggy Pop
sold out at the Pontiac Silverdome with my name up in lights.
Ten meters up, now a hundred now a thousand,
now two-hundred and twenty-three thousand meters
past the Karman line until I ain't
got the weight on my chest no more.

I got scars on my fingertips
that point to where the treasure lies. I got the
      keys to the city,
the keys to the kingdom.
I'm the reason why they changed all the locks.
I'm the reason you gasp with your body whole.
I'm a snake a desert rat crawling
the dry and dusty cracks
to come back to you
with my own blood in my mouth.
I'll snap my fingers and I will break your heart.
I will be returning with blood on the blade.

2.

Behind imperfectly closed doors
white paint sweating on the walls

I thought about the toil behind every grain of rice,
shadows that pass across the back of a cat asleep.

The man from Lubyanka follows me through Baikonur
mouth twisted pale like a wax-wane moon

stalking the iron rungs of the cathedrals,
of launching pads that bear the name

of my most beloved friends,
those who could never betray me.

seeking my own immortality,
I took the hand of the rabbit girl

    but it would never   come to hold.

Sitting cross-legged in the field
watching the ants up their ziggurats of dirt

carrying grains of sand
gingerly in their pincers

like it was the end of the universe
shall they falter, or fail—and I,

vengeful Hammurabi,
would snuff them out with my fingers.

One fell swoop like a prophecy.
I expect calamity, after all. Survivors

upside down my index finger,
the last to see their comrades alive.

Short summer days grant little mercies.
They never knew how close to death they were,

binary systems hardwired, a zero that flips
to a one.

    now the anthills dot the earth like so many polka dots
    now I live in the grass
    now I am become the golden patchwork
    now the blades wrap my limbs in twain

3.

they will tell of how I died:
powerless and cold
encoded in rust
cursing my native tongue until my blood vessels popped.
breaking promises to myself. how good were you
at saying goodbye? I ask,
my shame still on my lips.
oh, to place that distance
between us and the world below,
darkened sky eternal—
once I had (naively) asked for the stars,
and having now witnessed them,
they hardly compare
to the dazzling comets
of your imagination.

4.

the Politburo has spoken. the Premier will wrap
my memory inside ribbons of disinformation.

       Kosygin, that coward, has nothing left to say to me—
       get me on the horn to the Cosmodrome
       to curse this devil craft.

I am the signal flare from a sinking ship.
I am the first field ablaze when the Golden Horde comes.
I am the zigzagged line of red from an open mouth.
I am the dead language on the tip of your tongue.
I am the stick of dynamite under the bandstand.
I am a tin can silhouetted against the moon
a ghost who averts disaster by meeting it headfirst
but I shrink away like a leaf
or a shadow
to the wayside.

5.

someday, someday, they will
make a documentary about your life.

they will follow you through the mirage
of asphalt tinted yellow, a shiver

before a final stroke. any semblance of a breeze
is anointed by god. yet they fail to deliver their

forgotten mercies. this year you will forget about mercy;
but rather survival, tracing my many black-tarred snakes,

squiggly failures. in the film's final act
you filter slowly though a crowd,

take a deep breath, don't think too hard
and put on your breathing mask.

if I can't ever see you again
maybe I'll wash up in West Berlin

where the night sky reveals itself
a thick-fingered hand to lift my chin

skyward. to be lionized tomorrow
means nothing if you can't savor it today

try to reach your head above the waves
and grasp with your lungs for higher ground

look up: something's coming for sabotage
it's written in the stars

*There is something very elegant about throwing the
plates out the window after dinner,
and about living in a house that is
slowly sinking to its doom.*

-Tove Jansson

To All The Friends I Have Lost This Year

I wanted to scream in those unencumbered summer days,
burn the words down, smash all the printing presses,

feel the heat on my naked shoulders,
twirling off my tongue in neat little rows.

Can you uninvent a language? Erase this ungainly cuneiform
from color of dirt, scent of dry rock and concrete

filtering through the undergrowth. No volcano is truly dormant.

Heart-shaped oceans rising with steam heat,
waves colliding like galaxies. How quickly

the wrinkles form. How each image bounces
from one scene to another,

how they all line up somewhere near the end,
how my dead flowers appear like tendrils of squid ink.

Come the spring I plant them in the side yard,
stab the coinlike grubs with a hand rake,

then wait for life to come back
to the galaxies between our eyes,
the arch of your back like a suspension bridge.

But I simply couldn't
        find the words.

Am I floating or am I just tired?
Am I in control of this belly

full of sharpening swords
and my breath of sulfur and cat hair

whispering the true name of myself
to the buzzards who don't dare to speak

lest they fall from the sky,
spiraling through the dark hum

through seaweed underfoot
through signals received from deepest space

that only blue whales can hear.

Through the loves I can finally admit are loves.
Through questions unanswered and dispatches sent

and read
        to no avail.

through the force contained by my
fat and merciless cheeks.

Iron and rust through the bite marks.
Swallowing them like the syrup

my mother fed me when she felt the lumps
in my through her cold and bony hands.

Knowing that my only savior will be
the time it takes to heal my own blood,

the distance that ensues when I breathe deep,
        breathe deep,

pulling on my mask,
slurring the last words in my throat.

Cities In Dust

In this perfect howl of emptiness I conjure you

from blankets and linens and sheets of paisley,
your name perched gingerly on the tip of my tongue

seeking the words to describe your

alabaster body
hair of sandstone
navel lit aglow
and the looking-glass pool
where your ear meets your neck

but I never dared to speak,
my mouth rich with dead tongues
until you became a once-sweet thing
whose taste had worn out.

For days I couldn't sleep,
so concerned with survival
that I forgot to dream.

This was what I once wanted, to be
surrounded by reveries,

echoing across the hideous distance
between your words and my lips

like the gladiator who's made it this far,
kneeling on the ground of the amphitheater

searching for my missing limbs
clawing back the last few minutes of indecision.

I close my eyes to wake
in the ashen fields
hearing the long grass rustle,
sweet Herculaneum

where in the House of the Faun
I dream of making love to you,
wearing nothing but your hat.

Mareographe

the first doomed sailor
flinging himself headlong
into the tempest

flightless captive bird
last of its kind, still breathing
singing to a ghost

summer in July
the heat resides in your bones,
the stains on your dress

get so nervous I
pirouette like a gee bee
fabric wings on fire

soldiers raising their spears
in formation phalanx charge
emerging long night

Pleiades crash into
the last creatures left on earth
at mating season

what is it? you ask
and I can never answer
yet you have no mouth

Letter From The Williamsburg Bridge

Bad air blows in from Broadway-Lafayette,

drowning out the buskers and their electric violins

over sleeping tombs hoisted on water-rust rails

watching the rats squirm around pockmarked toes

searching for lost tunnels where the treasure may lie—

here and again I witness the marks

left scrawled among the sodden concrete

in some dream of this blackened earth.

Manhattan is a skyline is a towering cat

all choke and noise and steam and cough

with drums in its head steel thoughts in its mind

nestled in diners that hide in plain sight

where Marx sits at the piano and plays us show tunes,

where we aim our hatchets at police van windows;

where our dead memories fall by the wayside

among boxed wine and key lime pies.

Tomorrow in Bushwick we'll get

burgers and tiki drinks, bask in warm sunlight,

uncurling like soft petals—rosé and Mai Tais,

sundresses and hats and board shorts with anchors on 'em—

one last farewell in this season of wanting.

Apple of eyes, angel of dusk,

will you acknowledge my arrival

at the gates of this fabled city?

What do I say in the space between sentences?

Don't you find something delicious in apocalypse?

Don't you want to see how this all ends?

I can write you love letters until my fingers bleed

but it won't change a thing.

Good Luck Charm

a bird on a wire took a shit on my hand
as I sat next to you at Good Neighbor Pizza.

our legs were brushing each other.
missing our beers, it landed in the middle of the table

as if making an announcement

white and grey and black like dried house paint.
this bird staring at the top of our heads and motionless.

I washed my hands. reemerged from the cavern
and clinked beers with you

as you leaned against me
while I thought about luck

how it arrives on tattered wings:

    this manna from heaven
    narrow misses on my hand
    your leg against mine

Letter From The IKEA In Red Hook, Brooklyn

I was

imagining the future
I can never have

wandering ghostlike through
other people's homes. An accumulation

of lives hypothetical—cardboard televisions
and rows of fake books,

beautiful lilywhite strangers
staring back from RIBBA frames,

invented families conjured from scratch
and leading effortlessly into other rooms,

other families, other apartments, other realms,
like switching the television channel.

Follow the arrows.
Pathways like arteries

toward some great organ
like intestines arranged

flowing to some end
its conscious unknown,

yet working toward
the goal of keeping one alive.

—

I want people to hear my body scream
vibrating across these plasterboard walls:

tucked head-to-toe on a KLIPPAN couch,
below a LERHAMN stained antique,

curled up on a matte-black MALM
hugging my knees close to my chest

while young couples shuffle past
Sofas and Textiles and Wardrobe And Café

as my cat paws at an empty food bowl
and then at my face.

    Fuck it, I'll buy matching sheets in my favorite pastels,
    feel the combed-cotton bath towels,
    run my fingers on the low-pile rugs,
    touch the fuzzy leaves of artificial plants.
        Ingenious solutions
    and flatware storage and organizational designs
    for lighting fixtures and smarter men than I
        have engineered
    my kingdom where I hide like a stomping ghost
    haunting my fourth-floor walkup driving my
        neighbors insane
    with hammers and nails and slamming doors and
        midnight calls
    to the motherland. They will tell this to my landlord. I'll perish
        into the walls,
    I will dissolve in next year's heat. I'll smile at
        the employees

from behind my French Blue face mask. Please, keep your
    distance,
I've been doing it for years. If we now demand a
    faux sincerity
then listen, friend, I can provide that in spades.

In The Undergrowth

I sweep the dew across my fingertips,
drops of chalky water gleaming like

cubic zirconia tumbling from a velvet pouch.

we could have made it through
              this year
even if it killed us,
a year made rotten
with the cracking of knuckles.

in the throat of this earth
I listen to the end of the world
leaving dead messages in its wake,
wearing these grim moods
like a tattered suit that still fits.

a hunter's bullet pierces the sky.
a glass of Montepulciano.
a ruckus, a calling.
a flock of sparrows, ascending.

this soil was made to break my heart.

The Poisoner's Lament

That I was not there
to see my work
come to fruition.

That I was removed
from earthly relations
to my chagrin.

That I am at the mercy
of my naked prey,
their eyes wide as saucers.

Write down their names,
haunt them in their
loneliest hours.

Bring my knees up to my chest.
It is a great feeling
to make a plan.

But then no one will thank you,
no hands extended
to greet you at the dawn.

That I miss my cat.

I Am Not Young And I Will Die With This Car In My Garage
For Anne Sexton

1. On The Nature of Darkness

Everyone goes away, in the end.
It's a curious thing, this old box of bolts,
sputtering and clumsy with the smoke
of a thousand lost seasons,
it's a mouthful of dead languages
on the tip of your tongue. A set of
instruments that can't sense the hours,
needles shuddering as if they've been viewed
through a flickering light. A Cold War relic
dripping oil wherever it goes.

But I am more than just a pun on my name
from my 6th grade English teacher. Here,
    let me try again—
reborn as a cat in the hermitage,
surrounded by treasures
hanging on the tomb walls
and the pauper's graves. This could all be mine,
you say, particularly these sad bruised bones.
But I don't go to church anymore. I try not to drive.
I wake up hearing the neighbor
squirm and moan shaking the wall
with some new man she's got.
The cruelty is the point. To wander,
useless and afraid, lost in the archives,
filtering through bookshelves listening for breath,
jumping at the sound of unlocking doors.

Lift the hood skyward. See how its ink defies us

seeping like lost wax, hear its valves squirm
under the pressure we give it. Laugh lines across its
torn leather seats, maps to dead nations
lost and hidden from sight. We have always
demanded perfection. Give me another reason to break.

2. *Someone Had Climbed To*

the top of the bell tower. Evicted all the bats
with a broom handle. Scraped thin lines
into the ceiling above, where the mold once lay
thick and dripping with sarcasm.

But I am in the garden. Running my fingers
across bougainvillea I watch the fountain
burst into laughter, each drop of water a miniature planet,
gleaming like cubic zirconia spilled from a pouch.

Some might say that this is a lost year,
just one more lost year in this
great and grotesque world. But the dreams
stayed behind, refusing to answer us.

For all of those summer days I couldn't sleep,
jumping off balconies in Williamsburg.
Drowning in Tylenol on the howling trains
just to see if anyone notices.

Like you, I am tired of being brave.
Aren't you just so tired of feeling?
Don't you tire of the siren songs
to your own weariness?

The gap in the floorboards is a wound in my throat.
So concerned with survival that I forgot to dream.
How many existences scream from these stone walls?
Once I drew a snake with too many legs and I left it at that.

3. Angle of Attack

but you must remember that a car's interior
burns the brightest. smash the side window
with anything at hand—a wrench, a tire iron
a two by four you swing like Jackie Robinson.

soak the rag against the spout. take care not to spill.
through the window frame it'll catch in an instant
sweeping through torn leather, sunken foam:
heating up the seat coils like a burning stove.

have I ever steered you wrong?
after all, I am my mother's keeper.
you say I am capable of monstrous things.
and yet my heart's just not in it.

we Americans, too pessimistic
about the thought of death
view each ending as cause célèbre
as if we have never cried in private.

listen: the guillotine swish is the modern sound.
It is efficient in three distinct dimensions,
purity and precision, a well-weighted machine
with such grace that I weep at its elegance.

but loneliness is a birth condition

with no known cure.

and my demons

have caught up to me

like braying dogs.

67

I hope to see you out there someday. where we once
wrote letters to each other, letters for the future
keeping the generous ones close to us,
as long as your bravery lasts.

but until then there are no more innocents.
write down their names. leave nothing to chance
spit on your hands, know where your heart lies
know when to stay for the big show,

the bomb under the floorboards
ready for the final exit
the big finish

4. *Lament for Ivan Denisovich*

for a long time I woke up early. this morning in bed I read about Anne Sexton, and the marriage of Robert Lowell and Elizabeth Hardwick, and of Lowell's insanity, and the Christian martyrs Perpetua and Felicity, and Tadeusz Kościuszko, and the history of English muffins, and Herb Petersen (who invented the Egg McMuffin), and the movie *Chungking Express*, and the myth of the Wendy's SuperBar, and a recipe for Singapore-style noodles, and Richard "The Iceman" Kuklinski, and the Judeo-Christian mayor of Quincy, Massachusetts. I got out of bed. put my feet on the scratchy hardwood floor. felt like my stomach was churning with its lost equilibrium, hungry with the idleness, I just want to devour the world before I leave it. how can you expect a man who's warm to understand a man who's cold?

someday I shall be welcomed back to the land of the living.

5. The Destruction of Everything

My darling, the syrupy smell of death is
wild and young and free. Are you your blood

or your skin? You, formless, a cat like water,
who sinks teeth and claws

into my temples. I, unearthed from a sunken tomb,
a gift more trouble than what it's worth.

I am at the mercy of my prey. America is
a dead language, a tongue that bends

in half when you least expect it.
A people staring blankly in forgotten rooms,

waiting for some unmarked disaster,
they are cursed to remember everything.

This is how the first humans slept:
with rocks pressed to their temples.

But what is past never passes. For
not even god is allowed to touch you,

you false king of kings:
how quickly you've forgotten

the finery of your lifetimes
yet I still remember being

forever wounded like radiation,
striking the body long after spring's first blast.

I am my mother's burden.
Napalm in my kidneys

with the fuel rods spent,
I will always be your case study—

knees drawn to my chest
a corpse unfurled,

bathed in lightning,
bathed in heat.

Tongues wrapped
in barbed wire,

its life pooling at the base of your neck.

Gracie Square Hospital, Wednesday, August 5th, 2020

A stranger with pills in my stomach, I felt chain link fences rattling above my thin plywood bed I heard people running in sneakers out in the hallway like it was a parquet floor they were cheering and yelling and I assumed it was for blood I was asleep but lucid and I felt it all anyway. In the hallway and there was the usual clamoring in the distance the night shift on cheap chairs looking at videos on their phone the occasional fellow patients haranguing the people behind the nurse's station for supplies or for their clothes or for their psychiatrists who had all long gone home or just to ask if they could call out somewhere. A sleep aid for tonight, then Lexaprol in the morning. My roommate is an older Hispanic man named Felix in a red t-shirt and grey dreadlocks who sits at the side of the bed and stares blankly forward. He is sitting on the side of the bed when I enter to drop off my things and he is staring blankly forward when I brush my teeth in our little communal sink and he remains hunched over and staring when I climb under my sheets and take off my Jazzercise scrubs and ask him to turn off the lights. "No," he insists, "I have to sleep like this." In the past 24 hours bouncing between hospitals and squawking emergency rooms I had gotten an hour and a half of sleep. At one point I tried to sleep in the comfort room that is always locked with its big couch and its dimmable lights and its speaker and iPod nano that plays an endless stream of Enya until they finally noticed me and kicked me out. I ask a nurse if she could coax him into turning off the light. Her name is Robin and she is a dour middle-aged woman with thin round glasses. She says you can just turn off one set of lights the bottom set of lights might be easier for you and I try this and it's even brighter and I bury the pillow over my head half hoping I inadvertently suffocate in my sleep or at least succumb to a heart attack from the stress. The door opens with a bang and a nurse gazes in like a bored zookeeper and when she leaves I try to force the door shut and then she comes back and bangs the door open and yells at me that these doors can't be locked, every 15 minutes we gotta come to check on you. Woke up in the middle of the night to the most incredible snoring I had ever heard from a human being: like a bellowing steam engine of nightmares, like God's murder in my ears, like Optimus Prime passing a kidney stone. I make a plan to leave tomorrow. At 2:45am I asked for another pill and was given one. At 7:07am I did bloodwork. At 8:30pm I had breakfast scrambled eggs and cream of wheat livened with a thin packet of pepper which made me feel strangely hopeful for the future. At 9:04am I took my Lexaprol which made me feel strangely hopeful for the future. My roommate had been here for eight days.

The Birds

Birds die all the time, dropping out

of the sky. Maybe you just don't notice.

Their muscles stiffening, beady eyes fading,

they glide

gently, to the ground.

It is either the beginning or the end of the world, and the choice is ourselves or nothing.

-Carolyn Forché

I Am Checking In On You

to assuage my own guilt.
How are you? Are you doing well?
Are you drinking enough water?
Getting enough sunlight? Going
on walks? Have you tried meditation?
Good, great, thank you. But please,
spare me the details and your miseries,
your pleadings turned confessionals,
for though you treat them like such
your friends are not your therapists—
as if you pay them by the hour.
Your pity collapses the scaffolding.
Your veins are filled with drunk sloppy kisses.
Your spine is a sound tube in a dollar store:
flip it over and hear the sound of tomorrow.
You drink the sour wine.
The wine turns to blood. You apologize.
Once I had said the words to assuage your guilt
and you clung on like you believed me.

But now, nobody can accuse me of
looking the other way when you
slip into deeper waters,
as I still hold your hand
though I let it pass gingerly across my palms.

It must be said. I made an attempt.
An attempt was made,
A box checked,
A question asked,

but it was not the right one.
Your heart is a firing squad
and it denies you a final cigarette.

Boathouse on the Lullwater of the Lake

Some days I don't feel too bad.
Those days I find my way to the boathouse
at the faraway end of the old-growth wood
where I drown my bad thoughts in the pond
underneath its curled dry and yellowed leaves,
watch the mallards eat them
while a jazz band plays. Some days you don't feel
like an abandoned soldier wandering through the
finale of a spent apocalypse.
These days are frightening and unusual,
like the new weight of an arm that tingles
when it felt fine the day before. What is fine, really?
What is the worth of a present condition,
one that can be so easily forgotten/replaced?
My arm has hurt, my arm has always hurt like this.
On a 75-degree day in November under sinking leaves
the world looks
like this, the world has always
          looked like this.

Spring In Bloom: Two Haikus

everything we lost

can never hope to retrieve

    first sneeze of pollen
    blueberries in sangria
    windswept cotton dress

your hand holding mine

A Dream

Someday you will take an errant step in the tall grass and fall into

a realm where you are a king   But until then you check your
     pant legs for ticks

curse the dampness in your socks inhale resentment like wood
     smoke   Then venture forth

into the undergrowth   Someday under a red sky you will
     command the fog in the far trees

swirling like steam off an apple pie resting off a fairy tale
     windowsill   Write your art

in the steam of your breath until the light fades and your solitude
     like whiskey hugging you like

a cat that forgets its own size   Someday you will find the path
     through the woods that takes

you back to the front door of your noxious dreams   And you
     will knock.   And there will be

someone to welcome you with open arms and you will collapse
    like the black holes of a billion

stars a billion billion empty distances in your field of vision
    Limbs wrapped around each

other like the hydrogen-filled bladders of collapsing zeppelins,
    white-hot trellises of irony

where no steel-blued frost of winter can ever harm you

And you will wake up
and you will wake up.

AFTERWORD

Believe me, you have to believe me. You were put on this earth to break my heart in innumerable ways. I remember that little corner cafe where we used to go, the one where they served bottomless mimosas on Sundays, where we would pour big, tall carafes wet with melting ice into our glasses while raising our tall skinny flutes with our pinkies out in solemn sarcastic mockery: devour the rich, broil their skin until charred and crackling, burn their corpulent bodies for fuel, so we may stay warm through the night. Hopped fences to get here, bent and snarled, well-trod territory. Crossed the train tracks. All the people I once knew, the past friends I had, they've all gone. No sympathetic ear, no help to call upon. Man cannot live like a single man, tossed about by the wind. I can't rely on anyone's help any longer. I have to go out and do things to myself. It is a burden to receive these blessings as the last of my kind, still lashing my wings to the ground, to the soil below. I am old, I am ancient, I will be gone like a windswept dust. Who will talk to me when the parapets fall? Inheritor of apocalypse, where is your music now? You were put on this earth to break my heart in innumerable ways. Believe me, you have to believe me.

—

I Am Not Young And I Will Die With This Car In My Garage was written over a three-year period from Vermont to New York City and points in between. It was written primarily on a Vortex Race 3 mechanical keyboard with Cherry MX Blue switches and keycaps stained with red wine. I will never stop emphasizing how grateful I am to see these words in print: the only poetry I had ever published prior to this was in a children's anthology in 3rd grade. I had written about the cuckoo in a cuckoo clock. I believe the piece was titled "The Cuckoo In The Cuckoo Clock." My mother still has the anthology somewhere.

The absurd title is lifted verbatim from a Craigslist ad for a 1978 Lotus Esprit. Its honesty and heartbreaking nature struck me: it was a public admission of failure, like a mantra one repeats under their breath when they believe that nobody is within earshot. Get rid of your burdens before you feel old. We are all failing, constantly, 24 hours per day; we believe that we are getting ahead but even the Patrick Stewarts and Dolly Partons and Kazuo

"

Ishiguros of the world still believe that there is something more destined for them, just around the corner, lying in wait. The Lotus Esprit was bright yellow, and it had been sitting in a barn for nigh on 20 years, as old British cars tend to do. It was clearly more of a front lawn statement piece than one of the most daring cars ever created. Imagine waking up every day and walking past the door to the garage knowing that this totem to your failures is waiting inside and taking up space, brushing your kneecaps past the rust bubbles on its door just to take the trash out: a constant nag of your lost dreams, a tell-tale heart. Old car nerds always place too much emphasis on these things.

There is a fully-formed narrative one can piece together from these four sections; that must be open to your interpretations. I will I say this, however. In an era that would have been devastating regardless, it has been three years—one year of heartbreak, one year of failures, and one year of bloodletting. Trying to stay afloat. Speaking in tongues. Scrawling lyrics on out forearms in blood red pens. What was that quote from William S. Burroughs, about the title to his most famous work? Ah, yes: a frozen moment when everyone sees what is on the end of every fork. The world, in too stark a focus.

This era will serve as that fork. We choose our own ways out, and we leave something behind when we do. There is no pain, you are receding. Trust me, trust me on this. All of this. Someday I'll tell you all of this in person. May we both fare better than we already have. You have my love and my support.

Blake Z. Rong
Park Slope, Brooklyn
February 2021

ACKNOWLEDGEMENTS

I would like to thank the people who have believing in the idea that I could actually write something worth reading a damn. Namely: Nick Courtright, Albert Liau, and Cammie Finch at Atmosphere Press, Bianca Stone and Rita Banerjee of the Vermont College of Fine Arts, my classmate Lennie DeCerce, Joanna Fuhrman of Brooklyn Poets, Mark A. Murphy of *Poetica Review*, Clair Dunlap of *Vagabond City*, and Joanna C. Valente of *Luna Luna Magazine*. You all have made the writing world a less lonely place.

ABOUT ATMOSPHERE PRESS

Atmosphere Press is an independent, full-service publisher for excellent books in all genres and for all audiences. Learn more about what we do at atmospherepress.com.

We encourage you to check out some of Atmosphere's latest releases, which are available at Amazon.com and via order from your local bookstore:

Streetscapes, poetry by Martin Jon Porter

Feast, poetry by Alexandra Antonopoulos

River, Run!, poetry by Caitlin Jackson

Poems for the Asylum, by Daniel J. Lutz

Licorice, poetry by Liz Bruno

Etching the Ghost, poetry by Cathleen Cohen

Spindrift, poetry by Laurence W. Thomas

A Glorious Poetic Rage, poetry by Elmo Shade

Numbered Like the Psalms, poetry by Catharine Phillips

Verses of Drought, poetry by Gregory Broadbent

Canine in the Promised Land, poetry by Philip J. Kowalski

PushBack, poetry by Richard L. Rose

Modern Constellations, poetry by Kendall Nichols

Whirl Away Girl, poetry by Tricia Johnson

Blue, poetry by Gülru Gözaçan

ABOUT THE AUTHOR

Blake Z. Rong is the author of the nonfiction work *Beautiful Machines* (Gestalten, 2019). His short stories and poetry have appeared in *Poetica Review, Vagabond City, SLANT*, and *Isele Magazine*. A former automotive journalist, he has driven across the country four times. He currently lives in Brooklyn with a cat named Moose.

www.ingramcontent.com/pod-product-compliance
Lightning Source LLC
Chambersburg PA
CBHW021338060726
47591CB00006B/2086